CHIPPENHAM
THEN & NOW

IN COLOUR

MIKE STONE

The
History
Press

For Imogen, Jessica, Lennon, Lyla, Oliver and Sophie

First published in 2011

The History Press
The Mill, Brimscombe Port
Stroud, Gloucestershire, GL5 2QG
www.thehistorypress.co.uk

British Library Cataloguing in Publication Data.
A catalogue record for this book is available from the British Library.

ISBN 978 0 7524 6363 6

Typesetting and origination by The History Press
Production managed by Jellyfish Print Solutions and manufactured in India

CONTENTS

ACKNOWLEDGEMENTS

The contents of this book could have not been compiled without the help of Don Little, who gave me unlimited access to his Chippenham postcard and photographic collection; selected photographs were taken from his collection for this book. I would also like to thank the staff at Chippenham Museum and Heritage Centre, and Wiltshire and Swindon History Centre for assistance in research.

Finally a special thanks to my wife Marilyn and my son Alex for helping me to pull the book together.

ABOUT THE AUTHOR

Mike Stone is an active archaeologist and local historian in North Wiltshire. For eight years he was head of Archaeology and Heritage at Chippenham College, followed by ten years as curator of the Chippenham Museum and Heritage Centre until retirement in 2010. He is the author of three further books on Chippenham, including *Chippenham in Old Photographs* for The History Press. Currently continuing his research on North Wiltshire, he also edits books for a local Wiltshire publisher and, during the summer, carries out specialist heritage and archaeological guiding.

INTRODUCTION

The town of Chippenham, like most West Country market towns, has a long and varied history beginning with agriculture, then moving into the weaving industry and then cheese production. With the arrival of the railways in 1841 the town's fortunes were somewhat revived, especially with the establishment of four different railway engineering firms.

The new fashion of photography took hold in Chippenham in about 1865, both for family portraits and for views of the town's buildings and businesses. From 1865 to 1920 there were eleven different photographic studios, most of whom produced postcards that were purchased and sent from the post office to family and friends. The growing town of Chippenham also attracted photographic studios from nearby towns like Trowbridge, Melksham and Malmesbury. These photographs are often the only records we have of areas of the town centre and surrounding villages.

As the town continued to grow, many well-known structures and buildings began to be demolished, such as the fine old stone bridge over the river Avon, Mr White's Palladian house in the High Street, the Back Avon footbridge and Joe Buckle's fish shop. Two significant demolitions were the fine building on the corner of St Mary's Street, which became the present post office, and the well-loved Chippenham Cottage Hospital in London Road. One further effect of the population growth was the demolition of St Paul's School in Park Lane followed by the replacement of the large open-air swimming pool with the Olympiad Sports Centre.

With the increased population, who were mostly working at the railway factories, Nonconformist chapels grew in number, many with prominent positions on Station Hill and on Monkton Hill. From 1900 to 1914 further areas of housing were built to the north and west of the town centre, which were catered for by the building of new churches – the Church of England and the Methodist's church.

The town today is still growing and it is fortunate that many of the inhabitants appreciate and readily take up historic and conservation issues in order that the town can maintain what is left of its past heritage for future generations.

THE YELDE HALL

THE YELDE HALL, which has recently been totally refurbished by North Wiltshire District Council, is one of the last remaining medieval timber-framed buildings in the town and one of the two Grade I listed buildings of Chippenham. Archaeological investigations, which were carried out during the restoration, have dated the felling of the timbers to somewhere between 1446–58. The hall, which was originally used as a market with internal divisions, was constructed in the middle of the open market plain; until recently, it was thought to have been the only building in this area at that time. However, excavations within the Yelde Hall have revealed part of a very fine dressed-stone wall with a buttress, which may belong to an unknown early medieval building. The hall and its

upstairs room were used by the bailiff and burgesses for local government meetings. Underneath the chamber was the lock-up, or blind house, which was constructed of local stone quarried nearby. One of the earliest records is dated 1563 and refers to the key to lock the blind house door. In 1614 the bailiff's accounts show that the hall was renovated with new wood, roof, dressings and walls, which cost £7 2s 8d. A further intriguing record is dated 1709: the bailiff records in his accounts 'spent with six pirates in custody, one shilling for seven quarts of ale'. The photograph on the left dates to 1909, showing a building built against the Yelde Hall. The building was used by Long's Umbrella Hospital and Tobacconists. The owner, Mr Thomas Long, prided himself on having a wide selection of umbrellas and sunshades, and that he could repair any umbrella. In the 1950s the building was demolished to reveal the north wall of the Yelde Hall.

THE BUILDING IS now used as the town's Tourist Information Centre, which was opened in 2003. However, Chippenham Town Council is planning to move the Tourist information Centre and turn the building into the museum annex with the display of the town's historic fire engine.

CATTLE MARKET

THE OLD PHOTOGRAPH below, dating from about 1900, shows the Friday cattle market in full swing. Records show that ownership of the market rights was of considerable value to the lord of the manor, who also had control of the space in front of all premises in the Market Place. In 1765 all farmers in Chippenham were ordered to bring their corn, butter, cheese, turkeys, geese, chickens, pigeons, conies and eggs to sell in the public market. The market reached its peak in the reign of Queen Victoria, before the Board of Agriculture prohibited the selling of these goods from street markets in 1907 due to health risks. The Chippenham market later relocated to the rear of the Neeld Hall in 1910. In 1835 the bailiff and burgesses became the mayor

and councillors, before moving to the new town hall in 1841. The Yelde Hall then had a variety of uses, ranging from the Chippenham Savings Bank to the Chippenham Volunteer Rifle Corps, which was stationed here with its armoury from 1846 until 1911. The Chippenham Fire Brigade later took over the Yelde Hall and carried out changes to the building. The interior floors were levelled and re-laid to accommodate fire engines, and the end gable was cut to insert two large doors. In 1945 the fire brigade relocated to new premises in Dallas Road. In 1962 the borough council and North Wiltshire District Council reconsidered an earlier plan to turn the Yelde Hall into a museum, and after renovation work Councillor Mrs G.E. Moss opened the museum on 25 October 1963. The museum's collections grew and by 1999 it was bursting at the seams. It was relocated in 2000 to the old Magistrates' Courts. The renovated Yelde Hall has now reopened as the town's new Tourist Information Centre, with displays of the building's history.

RENOVATIONS HAVE RESULTED in the removal of the circular window above the door into the Yelde Hall. The doors have been replaced with ones designed to fit in with the fifteenth-century appearance of the building.

THE BUTTERCROSS

THE BUTTERCROSS IN around 1890, showing its plain Doric columns and the stone-tiled roof, which is in a poor state of repair. The buildings behind backed onto the Yelde Hall in the 1780s. Running along in front of the Buttercross and up to the corner where the old Waverley Café stood was a roofed building with no sides that contained a long bench on which all the slaughtered cattle, pigs and sheep were cut up for the nearby butchers' shops in the market. Unfortunately, this building burnt down and was not replaced. In 1889 Mr E.C. Lowndes bought

the Buttercross for £6 and took it to the grounds of Castle Combe manor where it was re-erected as a garden folly. The space left by the Buttercross was then utilised for a late Victorian building.

IN THE 1980s the Chippenham Civic Society had a vision to bring the Buttercross back to Chippenham from Castle Combe and to re-erect it in the Market Place. A successful fundraising project raised enough capital to purchase the Buttercross, repair and restore the structure, and re-erect it in the market plane. In 1993, after the North Wiltshire District Council pedestrianised the market plane, work was put in progress. During 1995 the Buttercross began to appear in the Market Place and now stands resplendent in the middle of the pedestrianised market area. The Buttercross is still extensively used on market days and by community charity groups from the town and surrounding area. After the removal of the Buttercross, a new Victorian building was erected on its site, which has had many different retail uses. The building has recently been cleaned and is currently used by an estate agent.

CHIPPENHAM STATION

WITH THE ARRIVAL of the Great Western Railway into Chippenham in 1841, customers approached the brand new station and admired the entrance and ticket office, which were built in an Italianate style. Due to the growth of the railways, Brunel's original entrance was enlarged

in 1858 using stone from the deposits near Box tunnel. The work was carried out by Rowland Brotherhood who had carried out extensive contracts for Brunel and whose railway works were on the other side of the railway line. The railway companies were nationalised in 1947 and the old Great Western Railway became the western region of British Rail. The old photograph on the left clearly shows the front station looking rather shabby, with sidings to the right. All this was to change when Dr Beeching published a report entitled 'The Reshaping of British Railways', which suggested the closure of about 2,000 stations and the withdrawal of 250 train services in the 1960s.

THE AREA IN front of the station was substantially changed with demolition of railway buildings and sidings. However, it was not until 2003–4 that the entrance to Chippenham Station was transformed with improved parking and access. The new layout was officially opened by Tony McNulty MP on 4 May 2004.

13

CHIPPENHAM VIADUCT

THE GREAT WESTERN Railway's chief engineer, Isambard Kingdom Brunel, designed the imposing classical railway viaduct and embankment, which was opened for use in 1841. The construction caused a great deal of disruption to the town and required the demolition of the Samborne farmhouse to the left of the old photograph below. The viaduct was built of Bath stone, which had been excavated from Box tunnel. In 1848 the viaduct was widened to accommodate

extra tracks when extensive use was made of bricks, which were probably made locally. To the left, behind the overgrown shrubbery is the front of Orwell House. In 1852 Rowland Brotherhood and his family moved into the house and added a large extension. In 1868 the family left and the house began its long association with retail; it is currently the Brunel, a bar and restaurant. The historic interiors have been preserved and can be viewed on entry.

THE AREA TO the right of the viaduct is still used to advertise the works of monumental masons, even though the cover building has now been demolished. The buildings viewed through the bridge were demolished as part of a road improvement scheme with pedestrian underpasses, which have since been filled in and replaced.

JOHN COLES

JOHN COLES ARRIVED in Chippenham from Birmingham in 1870 as a practising chemist, and quickly set up in business at No. 25 Market Place. He prospered and became heavily involved with the developing town, being elected mayor three times. He died in 1916 and left in his will £4,000 to be devoted to the cultural and educational advancement of the people of Chippenham. His legacy was invested and, with other loans, was used to purchase fifteen acres of parkland, which were opened to the public on 23 May 1923. The park contained a bandstand, children's

pool area, swings and a new bowling green. The old photograph shows members discussing a game, with a very low hedge behind suggesting that the photograph was taken not long after the park had opened.

TODAY THE CHIPPENHAM Park Bowls Club is thriving and the whole park is appreciated by a very wide audience. New attractions include a sensory garden, tennis and basketball courts and a millennium clock.

STATION HILL

THE DECISION IN 1837 to situate the new Chippenham Railway Station in its present position required land to be purchased and a road, called Station Hill, to be constructed. This was open land, much of which had been used as a saw mill and timber yard. One of the earliest buildings to be constructed was the sorting office in 1874, seen on the right of the photograph. Following the changes from horse-drawn service to motorised service in 1935, a small fleet of post office vehicles were kept at the site. With the continued growth of Chippenham, an extension to the sorting office was added in 1964.

THE SORTING OFFICE closed in 2008 and is awaiting development into apartments and a retail outlet. Below the sorting office was open ground until 1910 when a rollerskating rink was constructed. The large open space of the rink was used as a temporary billet for First World War soldiers prior to them embarking from the nearby railway station. By 1915 the popularity of rollerskating had declined and it became the garage premises of W.M. Burridge, which in turn became a motorcycle garage. Currently the building is empty and is becoming somewhat derelict. The trees were removed some considerable time ago, and, as can be seen in the modern photograph above, there have been few major changes to the standing buildings on Station Hill.

CHIPPENHAM COLLEGE

IN 1898 THE borough council received plans for a new Chippenham District Technical and Secondary School in Cocklebury Road. The project was overseen by Alderman John Coles and the chosen design was a scheme submitted by Robert Brinkworth, who worked for the Bath architect

Thomas Hall Silcock. The design, however, was amended due to financial constraints, resulting in a third of the planned school rooms being cut. Building work began with the laying of the foundation stone on 7 October 1899. The building costs were fixed at £3,500; the school was built of red brick with some use of Bath stone and the roofs were covered in green slate, which was later changed in favour of red tiles. The building was opened in 1900 and the first chair of governors was Alderman John Coles.

TODAY THE ORIGINAL buildings still have an imposing presence on Cocklebury Road but they are now somewhat dwarfed by a sprawling complex of added buildings culminating in a new wing, which was opened in 1992.

FOUNDRY LANE

THE ARRIVAL OF the railway in 1841 was followed just a year later by the construction of a new railway works on open ground by Rowland Brotherhood. After the collapse of Rowland's company in 1868, the company of Evans O'Donnell Ltd took over part of the old railway works in 1894 and began to extend to the north. In 1904 Evans O'Donnell joined with Saxby and Farmer Ltd. The old photograph shows employees leaving the works and walking down Foundry Lane. The gates

and chimney to the right show the location of Hathaway's Butter Churn Manufacturers, which utilised the old Brotherhood factory. The building to the left, called Clift House, was formerly a hotel run by Mr W.H.J. Cockram who also ran a greengrocer and florist's in the building to the left behind the trees.

CLIFT HOUSE IS currently used as offices. On the corner of the front wall is a plaque recording the end of Maud Heath's causeway. The Causeway was 4.5 miles long and ran from Wick Hill near Tytherton to Clift House. The buildings formerly occupied by Hathaway's were used by Westinghouse Brake and Signal Company in turn until the late 1980s when the site was sold and demolished. The area is currently a retail park that preserves the name of Hathaway's.

NEW ROAD

NEW ROAD IN about 1920 with Brunel's viaduct in the distance. The Edwardian neoclassical building to the left was built in about 1905 as part of a speculative development to improve the retail outlets in this area. The upper two floors were used as a tobacco factory, which was run by Mr Francis Holland. A large number of young girls were employed to hand roll thousands of cigarettes; one of their most popular products was a cigarette that was impregnated with

different perfumes. By 1919 the factory closed and was used as a stationery depot; later the Prudential Assurance Company used the factory as offices.

VERY FEW OF the other buildings on New Road have gone through major changes in appearance. The town house on the right was formerly the home of Mr Cullen, who ran the town mill. Later, Mr Cullen's house became a bank and is now the home of Goughs solicitors.

ORWELL HOUSE

LOOKING SOUTH DOWN New Road with Station Hill to the left. The buildings to the left were originally built as one whole unit, which, in 1908, was occupied by W.J. Ball & Son who specialised in home furnishings. The building to the right, heavily covered in ivy, was Orwell House, which dates back to about 1812 when a green field site was used to build a house for Mr John Provis. He was a substantial timber merchant whose yard was opposite on open ground until the Great Western Railway line was built and opened in 1841. The house next to Mr Provis's was built soon after 1838 and was called Cambridge Villa; it was occupied by Mrs Bramble. Mr Provis's house was later leased, and then purchased by Rowland Brotherhood and his family, who remained there

until 1875. By 1901 Mr Bardwell ran a school until about 1912, and the building went through a good deal of change after Mr A.R. Hinder extended the front to create a large shop to sell cycles. By 1935 the building was used by Barretts for selling house furnishings, until about 1993 when they ceased trading. In April 2000 the building was given a change of use and reopened as the Brunel, selling food and drink.

TODAY THE BUILDINGS to the left of New Road are mostly utilised for the supply of fast food. Orwell House is currently the Brunel, which is a restaurant and bar.

RIVER AVON

ABOVE IS THE view across the river Avon looking up River Street in about 1912. On the left of the photograph can be seen the new market stalls erected after 1910 when the market was relocated here from Market Place. Behind, the façade of the town hall can be seen in the High Street with a roof over the cheese market and corn exchange. Behind the central lower building was one of Chippenham's cloth mills, which were last used by Spiers as a silk factory until it was demolished in 1911. The buildings to the right were used as a slaughterhouse and, to the rear, a small bacon factory called the River Street Bacon Stores. The bacon factory was taken over by the

Wiltshire Farmers Limited Bacon Curing Company and later became the Avonvale Bacon Factory.

AS PART OF the redevelopment of this area, the buildings in River Street were demolished in 1974 to make way for a new Sainsbury's, which itself was demolished in 1996 and replaced by a new shopping precinct and car park.

BACK AVON BRIDGE

THE OLD PHOTOGRAPH below shows a view across the river Avon and Back Avon Bridge to the rear of the Nestlé factory. The buildings used by Nestlé were originally built in 1796 when Henry Burnet sold a lease on the land to Thomas Goldney. The Bridge Cloth factory in 1811 was described as having a dye house and shear shops. However, by 1830 the next owner, Anthony

Guy, was unable to make any revenue and was declared bankrupt in 1830. In 1831 Mr Joseph Spiers leased part of the factory until 1873 when the National Anglo-Swiss Milk Company acquired the site.

THIS AREA OF the river has been transformed with the erection of the weir, which, along with other water controls, was built in order to regulate the river to alleviate the flooding of the town. The two river islands of Rea and the Ham were substantially cut away to improve the river flow. The old Nestlé building has been refurbished and is currently being used as offices.

NESTLÉ'S MILK CONDENSERY

A VIEW ALONG Bath Road of the Nestlé milk factory (below). The condensed milk factory is probably the oldest condensery in England and was the first factory to have installed a modern stainless steel plant and machinery in 1935. The factory was the largest employer in the town and in 1905 a merger took place between the Anglo-Swiss and the Henri Nestlé company to become the Nestlé and Anglo-Swiss Condensed Milk Factory. The Swiss chalet-style building, known as Bank House, was built originally as the milk company's offices; when Bank House is compared to architects' drawings it appears never to have been fully completed. In the 1880s the Chippenham

factory was beginning to suffer due to strong competition from the Wiltshire United Dairies in Melksham, which was to become the giant Unigate Company. In 1897 the Anglo-Swiss opened a further factory at Staverton near Trowbridge, which is still in existence. Records of work at the factory survive and describe it as being extremely hard. Work commenced sharply at 6am and didn't finish until 7pm. In 1873 the ten-hour working day earned workers 4s a week. Workers were summoned by a single bell, housed on the roof of the factory in a small turret, which still survives. The well-known milk products from the factory were labelled 'Milk Maid sweetened condensed milk'. In the Second World War Red Cross parcels were packed at the Chippenham factory and despatched as far afield as Australia.

THE CONDENSERY FINALLY closed in 1962 when production was transferred to a new Nestlé factory in Cumberland. The east end of the factory was demolished leaving the main bulk, which was converted into an office; Bank House, after a period of neglect, has been converted into offices, whilst the large warehouses and yards behind are now one of the town's main car parks.

CHIPPENHAM BRIDGE

IN THE LATE 1950s Chippenham Borough Council embarked on a scheme to replace the old stone bridge with a modern one. In 1959 a pedestrian bridge was constructed from the edge of the old Co-op shop across the river to the Thomas Cook travel agent's. The old stone bridge was then removed in stages so that vehicles could have access as the new bridge was erected; the new bridge was officially opened on 2 May 1966. The large building advertising Redwood Brothers' stores was built some time after 1900 as part of the redevelopment of the area; opposite, a long row of new shops were constructed on the site of the mill, which was demolished in 1957. The people of Chippenham still talk affectionately of their missing stone bridge, however it has had a very chequered history, which is detailed in the borough council records. In 1613 William Bollyn was paid £3 16s for nineteen loads of hewed stone to make arches because part of the bridge had fallen down. In 1615

the bridge actually collapsed, and it was then not until 1641 that repairs were fairly advanced to bring the bridge back to public use. In 1684 the 'Great Frost' caused a build up of ice on the upside of the arches, and teams of men were employed to break it and push it through. Then, in 1796, the bridge was finally widened along its whole length, making it a suitable pathway for the ever-increasing traffic, after a meeting in the Yelde Hall resolved to spend a large amount of money on the project.

TO IMPROVE THE present flat concrete bridge structure ideas were put forward to create a more elegant design as a planned millennium project but this failed to attract any funding. A competition was held, and in 2000 the public voted on designs for replacement town bridge railings. The winning artist, Melissa Cole, designed arches that resemble the swirling river below. The railings were funded jointly by the old North Wiltshire District Council, Town Council and Westlea Housing Association.

THE HIGH STREET

THE HIGH STREET in the 1920s with the imposing Palladian revival house of Mr G.A. White can be seen in the old photograph below. The building may have been designed by John Wood the Elder of Bath in the eighteenth century. The building was originally erected at Bowdon Hill in about 1744 and later rebuilt at No. 24 High Street, Chippenham. The building was demolished in 1932 by Blackford & Sons of Calne, with William Rudman acting as site architect. The building was skilfully taken down and re-erected at No. 1 Sion Hill, Bath, which is now part of Kingswood School. It has been described as

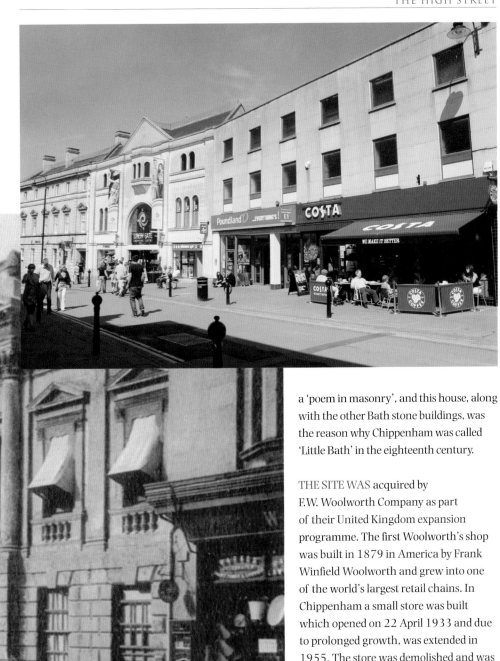

a 'poem in masonry', and this house, along with the other Bath stone buildings, was the reason why Chippenham was called 'Little Bath' in the eighteenth century.

THE SITE WAS acquired by F.W. Woolworth Company as part of their United Kingdom expansion programme. The first Woolworth's shop was built in 1879 in America by Frank Winfield Woolworth and grew into one of the world's largest retail chains. In Chippenham a small store was built which opened on 22 April 1933 and due to prolonged growth, was extended in 1955. The store was demolished and was rebuilt in 1975 with a very flat and bland exterior. The company went into a decline and the store was closed on 3 January 2009; the large store was then divided into three separate retail units, two of which are now occupied.

RIVER
STREET

LOOKING DOWN RIVER
Street in about 1906 towards
the river and Back Avon
Bridge (right). The street was
formerly known as Back Lane
and had a concentration of
manufacturing businesses
and public houses. Towards
the top was the Lamb public
house, which dated back to
before 1629, and further down
was the Swan or White Swan,
which was known locally as
'Paddy's Goose'. The Swan
was certainly in existence
before 1784 but by order of the

borough council it was pulled down in 1912 to make room for the relocated cattle market. The new brewery, run by Mr Slade, was started here, as was the Aerated Water Manufactory of S. Smart and John Merritt. Between 1973 and 1974 the whole area was demolished to make way for the new town centre extension.

SADLY, THERE IS now only one original building still standing at the top end of River Street, which is a Christian book shop. Most of the demolished area of River Street is now occupied by the precinct car park.

THE HIGH STREET
CONTINUED

THE VIEW BELOW looks up the High Street to a row of timber-built buildings, which were probably originally built in the Tudor period. The buildings have a long association as the ironmonger's

shops of Lines and Leonard, a company that was established in 1761. The company was then taken over by Mr G.E. Ireland, who then sold it to Mr Albert Blackford who used the building until 1908 when it was demolished.

A NEW BUILDING with an imposing stone façade and brick sides was erected late in 1908. In the 1960s it was occupied by the International Stores, which later became the International Supermarket. A variety of other retail outlets have used the ground-floor shops, which have recently been redeveloped and upgraded.

ST MARY'S STREET

VIEW LOOKING TOWARDS the corner of St Mary's Street with the Market Place. The large town house on the corner was originally a public house called The Boot, which was in existence in 1703 but had closed by about 1750. The building was then developed as a wealthy cloth maker's house, which by about 1830 had been converted into shops. The house next door was The Seven Stars public house, which became the chemist shop run by 'Doc Couch'; the owner William Couch was also called 'Doctor Tonic' or simply 'Doc' and he was one of the first chemists to start making and selling specific medicines for specific ailments rather than the 'cure-alls' of the nineteenth century. In 1951 the chemist shop and neighbouring buildings were acquired by the government and were demolished to provide the site for Chippenham's new post office.

THE POST OFFICE was designed by C.G. Pinfold and was officially opened on 10 June 1959 by Sir David Eccles who was both president of the Board of Trade and MP for Chippenham. This is still the main post office for Chippenham, however plans have been drawn up to utilise large parts of the building for other purposes.

CHIPPENHAM COTTAGE HOSPITAL

BELOW IS A VIEW across London Road of the Chippenham Cottage Hospital in about 1930. The cottage hospital was designed by Graham Awdry, an architect who had his practice in Westminster, London. Construction began in 1897 and it was officially opened in 1899. It was built of red brick with a Roman-style tiled roof fronting directly onto the London Road. In 1932

the hospital board decided to add a ward for women, which was designed by Walter Rudman of Chippenham. Later, in 1936, a nurses home was added to the rear. The hospital governors worked very closely with the Chippenham community as they were constantly in need of funds. After the First World War there were numerous fêtes held in John Coles Park to raise money, which led in 1923 to the first Chippenham carnival, which became the main fundraiser for the hospital for many years. The hospital was administered by Chippenham & District Board and later by the Mid Wiltshire Hospital Management Committee until 1974.

THE HOSPITAL BEGAN to decline in use and in the 1990s it was finally demolished and was replaced by houses fronting onto London Road and in the new areas of Larkham Rise and Royal Oak Close.

45

ST PAUL'S
NATIONAL SCHOOL

WITH THE CONTINUED growth of the population in the Park Lane area of Chippenham, St Paul's National School was built and opened in 1857. A government Treasury grant of £776 was made towards the total cost of £1,900. The architect was Henry Weaver of Calne, who designed the school and schoolhouse in the Gothic revival style. In 1926 St Paul's National School was transferred to the county council and in 1927 it was a school for infants only.

IN 1975, DUE to the continued growth of Chippenham, a master plan was drawn up resulting in a new St Paul's Infants' School being built in Greenway Lane and opened in 1972. The old St Paul's school buildings were demolished and replaced with a row of houses and flats along with the retained schoolhouse.

THE CHIPPENHAM SWIMMING CLUB

THE CHIPPENHAM SWIMMING Club, which was founded in 1877, is possibly one of the oldest swimming associations in the west of England; the club used the river near Long Close and one of their long term goals was to have a purpose-built swimming pool. From 1948 bathing in the river was considered unsafe so the members were forced to travel to Devizes pool, there was, therefore, great joy when the council announced that a new pool was going to be built on land adjoining the river Avon in Monkton Park. Monkton Park Swimming Pool was officially opened to the public on 25 May 1960 by the mayor, Councillor R.G. Archard, with displays of diving by the ladies' section of the Bristol Central Swimming Club, the Swindon Dolphin Amateur Swimming Club, and the Cheltenham Swimming Club, with assistance from the Chippenham Amateur Swimming Club.

The pool was 165ft long and 60ft wide, with a 12ft diving pit. These standards allowed it to be used for national competitions. The pool contained 360,000 gallons of water that were filtered through the treatment plant, which could clean the whole of the pool in four-and-a-half hours. The swimming pool was open from May until September and was very popular with the people of Chippenham. All the local schools attended the pool for swimming lessons. The cost of admission ranged from 1s 6d to 2s for adults and from 6d to 1s for children up to fifteen years old. During the pool's heyday in the 1960s and '70s, thousands flocked to the pool for sunbathing and swimming.

THE NORTH WILTSHIRE District Council embarked on a scheme to build the new Olympiad Sports Centre, which incorporated an indoor pool for all-year-round use. After the opening of the new pool in 1989 the district council proposed to close the open-air pool due to spiralling maintenance costs. Petitions were organised but it was a referendum among the town's rate payers that indicated there was insufficient support to run the pool and it was therefore demolished, leaving many people with only their happy memories of the large outdoor pool. Where the pool once was is today part of Monkton Park recreation area. However, during very hot, dry summers, the shape of the pool can be observed from the air as a parch mark in the grass.

THE ANGEL HOTEL

A VIEW ACROSS Market Place in 1904, looking towards the Angel Hotel, which was one of the main coaching inns in Chippenham, can be seen below. In 1613 it was originally called the Bull, before being changed in 1737 to the Angel. The façade dates to the eighteenth century and masked some of the earlier parts, which date back to the seventeenth century. Prior to 1751 the author Tobias Smollett stayed in the Angel Hotel, where he observed a chambermaid on whom he modelled the mother of his hero in the novel *Peregrine Pickle*. He again stayed in the Angel Hotel, and used it as a setting for part of his novel *The Expedition of Humphrey Clinker*. In the

Angel a Glamorgan gentleman called Matthew Lloyd has a brief liaison with a barmaid, the end result being the birth of Humphrey Clinker. In 1780 the Angel was run by James Hanson with the *Bath Chronicle* listing its attractions as '20 beds, good horses, post coaches and chases'. Around 1800 the Angel was run by James Younge, who also ran a small post office inside. The balcony over the porch was used by prospective members of parliament for election speeches. At the election of 12 July 1865 speeches were being made by the elected members Sir John Neeld and Sir Gabriel Goldney. A large crowd became enraged and pursued Mr Goldney across Market Place, after his escape the rioting took hold and was only quelled when a company of Coldstream Guards were billeted in the town. Originally there was stabling for the coach horses and visitors behind the Angel Hotel, but this was all swept away in 1958.

IN 1959 THE architect R.J. Brown was commissioned to build one of the earliest English versions of American motels. These too have been demolished and the hotel has had an extensive refurbishment and redevelopment to the rear. It now has additional hotel rooms, a health centre, gardens and new bars.

CHIPPENHAM BRIDGE

LOOKING ACROSS THE stone bridge, up the High Street in about 1912 (right). The building on the right stands on a small island and is referred to as Higgins House. The house was originally built as a tollhouse with a barrier to raise funds for the upkeep of the bridge. With the removal of the turnpike barrier, the Higgins family carried out the joint business of ironmongery and confectionery from 1870 to about 1908. By 1910 the shop had changed to the watch-making business of W. Buckeridge and later of Sebastian Palmer. The remaining part of the building was used from 1910 by H. Bowel and Co., newsagent and stationer. The buildings were demolished, along with the bridge, in 1957. The fine stone balustrade was added when the bridge was widened in 1796. Further up on the right is the square building known originally as the Bridge Inn; the inn closed and was acquired by Mr H.J. Pond who ran a grocery store for about eighty years along with a wine and spirits business.

THE BUILDING WAS demolished in the early 1960s and was rebuilt and opened as a Burtons supermarket, which in turn became a Fine Fare and is presently a Superdrug store with a hairdressing salon above.

THE SHAMBLES

THE OLD PHOTOGRAPH opposite looks along the pedestrian street called Ye Olde Shambles in about 1890. The area originally was open ground forming part of the market plane with the Yelde Hall being the only standing structure. From the late sixteenth century butchers began to set up temporary stalls here, which over time became permanent structures. Records suggest that on market days local butchers were joined by butchers from the villages to receive the animals that had been sold on market days. The buildings with the high gabled roofs suggest that they were all built of timber frame with wattle and daub roofs. Behind the building on the left was the site of the Three Cups inn, which later changed its name to the Shambles Hotel and then the Talbot Hotel, which closed in 1966 and was demolished in 1968 to provide a site for the new Barclays Bank.

THE SHAMBLES TODAY preserves its back walkway. However, there are no longer any shops fronting onto the Shambles.

THE MARKET PLACE

THE MARKET PLACE on a non-market day. On the left is the Duke of Cumberland, which prior to 1750 was known as the Trooper. Next are the spirit vaults and on the end is the King's Head Inn, with St Andrew's church hidden behind Smalcomb's furniture removers. The business was founded by Edmund Henry Smalcomb, who was born at Bremhill in 1847. He was described in the census of 1881 as a furniture broker master and he sold all aspects of household furnishings but would also carry out repairs, lay linoleum and dabbled in antiques, shot gun ammunition and fishing tackle. The added eighteenth-century façade of Smalcomb's hides the Tudor box-frame building. In 1613 this building was occupied by the Lyon inn. An interesting story is often told that in early 1666 John Woodman is supposed to have plotted with others to start what became the

Great Fire of London – a good story but with little credence! In the middle of the market plane is the fountain, which stands on the site of the town well and pump, which was falling into decay by 1867. In 1877 the borough formed a drinking fountain committee and invited designs for a new granite fountain to be erected at the cost of £200. The favoured design was by Mr W. Galsworthy Davie, architect of King William Street, London. The fountain was built of red and grey granite with a lower basin used for animals on market days. The fountain was built during the winter of 1878, and with the move of the town's market the fountain essentially became just a decorative item. Following the First World War and after a public subscription, half of the fountain was cut away and the town's new war memorial was built. The memorial was unveiled at 3pm on 4 September 1921 in front of a huge congregation of Chippenham people.

THERE ARE VERY few changes to this fine view today with the tower of St Andrew's church dominating the area. Most of the changes have been made to ensure smooth traffic flow through the town, and one has to cross busy roads to stand and inspect the fountain and memorial today.

THE CAUSEWAY

THE OLD PHOTOGRAPH below shows The Causeway in about 1910. On the right is the Five Alls public house, which is one of the few timber houses in Chippenham still to retain its jetty. Records suggest that the Five Alls may go back as far as the Stuart period. The Five Alls stand for 'I rule all', 'I fight for all', 'I plead for all', 'I dress all' and 'I pay for all'. In 1823 'I dress all'

was changed to 'I work for all'. In 1937 the licence was surrendered when the new Five Alls was opened in Sheldon Road. The building, prior to becoming a Chinese restaurant, contained on the upper floors remains of a hand-painted decoration, and to the rear there are still remains of a dovecote. The building on the left is a mock Tudor building, which for many years was a sweet shop.

VERY LITTLE HAS changed in this view of The Causeway, with many of the buildings being tastefully renovated. Surveys have shown that many of them contain elements of timber architecture from the fifteenth century.

LONDON ROAD

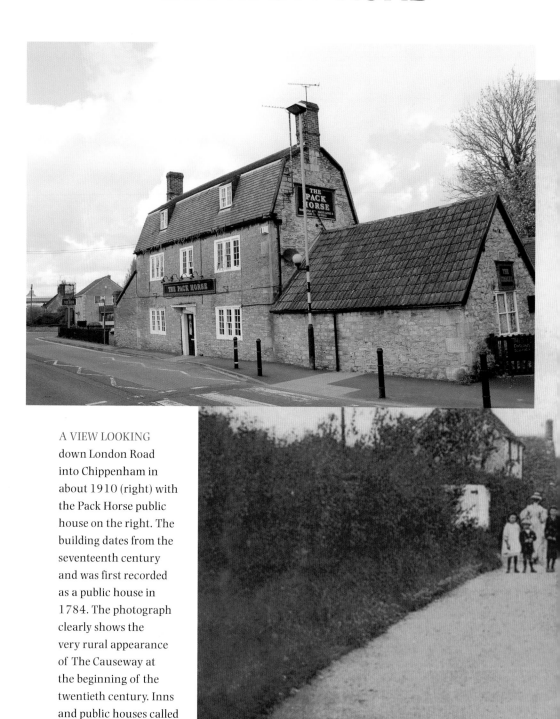

A VIEW LOOKING down London Road into Chippenham in about 1910 (right) with the Pack Horse public house on the right. The building dates from the seventeenth century and was first recorded as a public house in 1784. The photograph clearly shows the very rural appearance of The Causeway at the beginning of the twentieth century. Inns and public houses called the Pack Horse were normally on the outskirts of market towns to cater for the pack horse drivers and drovers during market days.

THE PACK HORSE today is part of a long ribbon development of buildings along the London Road with growing estates on either side.

MALMESBURY ROAD

THE VIEW BELOW, looking up Malmesbury Road, dates to about 1910. On the left is the Little George inn, which was rebuilt in 1903. The earlier Little George inn was originally built some time around 1784 and was much smaller in scale. The inn takes its name from King George III, and there was also in the High Street a public house called Big George, which takes its name from King George IV who was overweight! The inn was on the very edge of the borough boundary and

opposite the turnpike gates. Its trade grew rapidly with the creation of railway engineering opposite. In the early morning of 20 December 1903 the Little George inn was totally destroyed by fire. The rebuilt inn was designed by H.W. Matthews. With the opening of the new inn the local newspaper described it as a most 'handsome and commodious hotel with bed and bath', all built to a very high standard including art nouveau fireplaces, an expensive semi-conical roof and vast amounts of Bath stone. There was also extensive stabling at the rear, which was all demolished in 1970 to make a new link road from Park Lane to New Road. On the right is St Paul's church, which was designed by the nationally famous architect Sir George Gilbert Scott. The building was started in 1853 and was finally completed in 1861 with a tower and spire measuring 176ft high.

THE ONLY CHANGE to this area has been the creation of a new mini traffic roundabout where the lights used to stand.

STATION HILL CONTINUED

LOOKING UP STATION Hill in about 1912. On the right is the imposing façade of the Station Hill Baptist church. The church was built in the new station road and was officially opened on

6 May 1856. The building is built in a very charming classical revival style with a large pediment and pilaster columns. This style was heavily adopted by Nonconformist architects who had fallen under the spell of classical architecture from the 1840s to the 1880s. In 1930 the church was revamped with the removal of the old boxed-in seats. New lighting, rostrum and a new organ were also added.

THE BAPTIST CHURCH still dominates the bottom of Station Hill because of its imposing classical style.

THE NEW
WESLEYAN CHURCH

THE NEW WESLEYAN church on the slopes of Monkton Hill was erected on the site of the Black
Horse inn, which was first recorded in documents in 1784. Nearby was a small pottery workshop

producing earthenware pots for sale in the town. The land was bought in 1900 and was cleared and excavated between 1902 and 1903 by the men of the church. The building was opened in 1909 and was intended to mark the centenary of Methodism in Chippenham. The style is classical with a plain pediment and half engaged columns on the front with pilasters on the sides. The slope of the hill resulted in the church being built on a podium, giving it a very dominating position overlooking the river Avon. With the closure of the Methodist church on The Causeway in the 1980s a number of worshippers moved to Monkton Hill church, which was renamed as the Central Methodist church.

THERE HAVE BEEN renovations in the church from the 1980s and recently, and these have increased the size of the building to the side and rear.

THE PRIMITIVE METHODIST CHURCH

THE PRIMITIVE METHODIST church in Sheldon Road was constructed in 1901 with a seating capacity of 250. In 1932 it became the Sheldon Road Methodist church. Further groups of members joined in 1980 after the closure of the Cause Methodist church. A schoolroom was constructed, and in 1968 a second school room was added to the rear. Further work was carried out in 1989, which, in 2009, was demolished allowing the public areas and schoolrooms to be reconstructed as part of the Beacon project. The row of houses behind the church were constructed some time after 1900 with some of the rows being named after the Battle of Omdurman (2 September 1988),

Sudan Terrace (after the military campaigns) and Sirdar (an Eygptian/Melik Society term for 'a leader of the army' given to General Kitchener). The other side of the road was open country made up of orchards and grassland. This was all earmarked by the borough council for future development. The Ladyfield estate was constructed by W.R. Osborne of Swindon, and by 1914 up to forty-five of the planned 220 houses had been constructed.

THE LEFT-HAND side of the road has now been extensively built up since the 1920s – completely changing the once rural aspect of this side of Sheldon Road.

UTTERSON FOUNDATION

IN 1884 ELIZABETH Utterson left a foundation deed with money to erect five cottages in Lowden, with instructions that four of them should be used as homes for elderly ladies. Land to the side of the almshouses was purchased for £160 in 1885 for the building of a new church for Lowden. The new church was designed by Graham Awdry and was built by Messrs Light & Smith of Chippenham at a cost of £1,095; the bricks for the construction of the church came from the brickyard near Audley Road. The church was dedicated on 19 October 1886 by the Archdeacon of Bristol, Canon Norris. The church was serviced by the vicar and assistant curates of St Andrew's church until 1905. In 1961 discussions were again commenced to consider building a new church to take account of the new estates and increasing population. On 27 June 1967 the foundation stone for the new St Peter's church was laid by Oliver Lord Bishop of Bristol on the corner of Lord's Mead and Frogwell. In 1968 the congregation moved to the new church, leaving the old St Peter's to become the New Testament Church of God.

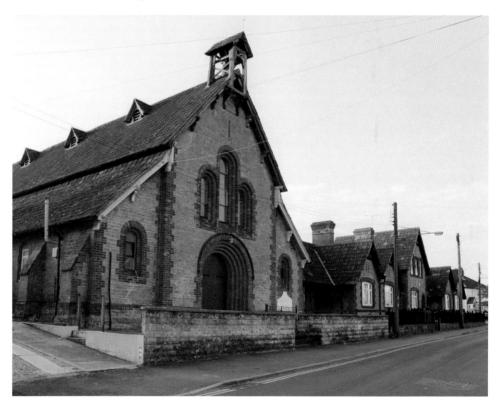

THERE HAVE BEEN few changes to the church over the years except for the remodelling of the bell turret and the removal of the rather untidy front fences. The Utterson almshouses continue to be used as they were intended.

MARKET PLACE

LOOKING UP FROM the High Street into the Market Place in 1905 (right). On the left of the photograph is the Royal Wilts Bacon shop, originally occupied by the Kettle public house, which burnt to the ground in 1839. The large imposing shop to the right was occupied by the Stevens family who ran a boot and shoe business from 1878 until the business closed in 1916. Just after 1920 the building was demolished and a building put up in the Edwardian classical style for

use as the Midland Bank. The house with the bay windows to the right was a town house, which, on the death of the owner, was purchased and demolished for the erection of the new Burton's men's clothing store. The foundation stone is inscribed with the names of both Raymond and Arnold Montague Burton, with a date of 1937.

THE HIGH STREET and the Market Place have now been pedestrianised and are often filled with market stalls on Fridays and Saturdays. A recent addition by the town council are large planted trees, which make the area look vibrant.

THE OLD POST OFFICE

THE OLD PHOTOGRAPH below shows the north side of the Market Place, with the second post office at No. 50, which was opened in the 1870s. The earliest records of a postal service in Chippenham date to the late sixteenth century and refer to post horses used for the relay of mail between London and Bristol. With the introduction of mail coaches in the eighteenth and

nineteenth centuries the postal service was sped up, the early post office being within the Angel Hotel. The arrival of the railways severely cut the mail coach service and the post office was relocated to No. 6 High Street before moving to No. 50 Market Place, as shown in the photograph. In 1874 the postmistress was Mary Elliot and she had fourteen staff. There were many deliveries each day and the post office was open from 7am to 10pm! The outfitters Hutchings was trading in the 1870s and the business closed in the 1930s. Further up the road was Heath the draper, costumier and milliner.

THERE HAVE BEEN few changes to the buildings on the junction of the High Street and Market Place. Towards the top of the street can be seen the new post office, which was built and opened in 1959.

SAMUEL
SPINKE

SAMUEL SPINKE SET up his printing works
and shop in 1858. As the business expanded
he took over a redundant Baptist church in The
Causeway and turned this into his printing works.
He advertised his business as being 'the largest
and best equipped printing works in the district',
his regular adverts emphasised his wide range
of services ranging from providing artistic copy

to supplying large commercial contracts. He also became a book seller, a book binder and book repairer. Like a lot of other Chippenham businesses owners, he ran a second business being the agent for the Royal Line of Canadian Northern Steam Ships operating from Bristol to Canada. Samuel Spinke was always up with the latest technology and, after a refit of his works, in 1909 he produced his own little booklet showing the interior with his gas-powered machinery printing works. The most useful of all of Spinke's products are the local directories of Chippenham traders and the community, which he produced from about 1870 to 1920.

THE BUILDING THAT housed Spinke's has changed little today, maintaining all of its earlier architectural details in the pediment above the door. The building has since been painted white and is now used by an estate agent.

PARK LANE

WITH THE IMPROVEMENTS in the late nineteenth century around the top end of Park Lane and the Little George inn, a wide range of small retail outlets began to appear. At No. 28a Mr W.G. Powell set up as a tobacconist and also ran, in the back of the shop, a hairdressing business along with the manufacturing of umbrellas. The photograph on the right shows Mr W.G. Powell standing in front of his shop in about 1912. The shop was purpose built and had some very bright green tiles around the shopfront. In the mid 1920s the shop changed hands to the Tompkins who continued the business for nearly thirty years.

IN THE 1950S Reg and Evelyn Pugh took over the business, followed in 1968 by R.F. Candy, who added a wide range of confectionary to the tobacco business. With the decline in tobacco sales, the shop ceased trading in 1988 and has been used for the sale of records, fireworks and facial massage. The shop is now empty but the bright green tiles have survived the years.

CO-OPERATIVE STORES

THE HIGH STREET can be seen below in about 1920, with the Co-operative Stores on the right. In 1844 a group of twenty-eight Rochdale cotton mill workers established the first modern co-operative, the Rochdale Equitable Pioneers Society, and aimed to combat high food prices by pooling scarce resources and buying at a lower rate. The four items they started with were flour, oatmeal, sugar and butter. Every customer of the 'co-op' became a member, having a true stake in the business with a share later paid out as dividends. The co-operative opened in Chippenham

in the 1890s, the first manager being Mr G.A. Geddes. The shop prospered until the 1990s when a decline set in and the store closed. Today the store is occupied by Wilkinson who, like the co-operative, offer cut-price products. Opposite can be seen the archway with the town coat of arms above it. The archway lead down to the cattle market that was here from 1910 until 1954. Next to the arch is the large town hall built by Joseph Neeld in 1834. In 1850 the area behind the town hall was expanded to include a cheese and corn exchange, which is now called the Neeld Hall.

APART FROM THE loss of Mr White's classical building, the buildings of the High Street have changed very little over time, as can be seen from the 2011 photograph above.

HIGH STREET CONTINUED

CHIPPENHAM HIGH STREET in about 1902 (below). On the left, with its two tall Tudor gables, is the fish and poultry shop at No. 17 High Street. In 1899 Joe Buckle formed a partnership with his brother-in-law Walter Hiscock to buy and sell fish and poultry. Joe's enthusiasm and dedication transformed the shop, particularly when the shop was dressed for the Chamber of Commerce window dressing competition; Joe won the competition so many times that he was eventually given the trophy outright. He also embarked on national window dressing competitions and won

some of these as well. After Joe's death in 1950 Hubert Ashman took over the shop until he retired in 1960. Slowly, through lack of proper maintenance, the shop fell into decay, and was eventually demolished in 1963. Even today, many people regret the loss both of Joe's business and the building sometimes affectionately referred to as Chippenham's 'little Harrods'.

THE DEMOLISHED SHOPS were replaced with a two-unit Bath-stone building. In the 1960s the buildings running down the High Street from Joe Buckle's old shop were in a fairly squalid state. Developers moved in, maintaining the façades but completely rebuilding behind. There was little recording of what was demolished apart from films made by the Chippenham Movie and Video Club, which showed elements of buildings dating back to the Tudor period.

THE CAUSEWAY
CONTINUED

THE CAUSEWAY IN about 1910 (below), the area to the left was used as a builder's yard and may also be the site of a recorded small brickmaker's yard, the buildings to the right have changed

very little apart from ground-floor shops being converted back to private dwellings. After the First World War Burlands Road was cut to the left linking onto Wood Lane and after the Second World War the yard was developed as a garage, which today is run by the Vauxhall Motor Company.

THE CAUSEWAY IS one of the longest highways in Chippenham and was referred to by name in 1603, however it may have had a name change and could have been called Langstret from 1245 due to its length. During the last ten years, residents of The Causeway have been restoring and cleaning the fronts of the buildings, some of which have won Civic Society awards. Many of the old shops have also been converted back to domestic occupation but retain elements of their shopfronts.

THE COMMON SLIP

THE 1926 PHOTOGRAPH below shows the Common Slip looking towards the river Avon. There is good evidence to suggest that the Common Slip has existed for centuries to allow the Chippenham families in this area access to the river Avon to launch boats, cross the river and wash their clothes. It is quite common when houses line the riverbank for the borough to provide access to water. The name is fairly unusual and other examples only exist at

Bucklers Hard, Hampshire and Portsmouth. In 1710 a plan of Monkton House opposite shows a landing point, and the owners may have had their own private ferry. Before the weir was built downstream, in the summer the river could be forded, and local tradition has it that animals were also walked down to the water on a regular basis.

THE COMMON SLIP lines up with Ladds Lane, which some historians argue is the edge of the Saxon defences laid out in the ninth century, if this is so then the Common Slip is one of the oldest surviving access routes to the river. There have been few changes to the area since the 1926 photograph apart from the planting of some trees near the river's edge.

PARK LANE CONTINUED

LOOKING UP PARK Lane in about 1904 (right). Originally the lane was called Little George Lane and consisted of a rutted narrow access leading from open country up to the Little George inn at the top, with ongoing access to the old road, until it was cut by the railway in 1841. In 1857 the Reverend Robert Ashe gave land for the building of St Paul's National School, which was then called Parish Road. With the continued growth of Chippenham's population, linked to the growth of the railway works, both sides of Park Lane were built up between 1890 and 1901. The lane was then widened and renamed Park Lane in 1893.

THERE HAVE BEEN few changes to the buildings in Park Lane, which remains a pleasant residential street. The only major difference between the street in 2011 and in 1904 is the increase in traffic and the parked cars which line the road.

HARDENHUISH ESTATE

WITH THE COMPLETION of the north side of Park Lane, further expansion began to the north and on the south side of Hardenhuish Estate with its open parkland. The old photograph

PARKFIELDS. CHIPPENHAM.

(left) of Parkfields looking west shows the houses just after their completion in about 1905, with gas supplied by the Chippenham Gas Works. On the right is a pile of kerbstones that have yet to be positioned. The location of these houses again suggests that they were built for workers who were employed at the nearby railway engineering works.

THE SOLID SEMI-DETACHED houses with their red roofs have changed very little since their construction in 1905. The main change is that most of the house owners now have cars that they can park in the front of their homes. Note that the attractive gas lamp no longer stands on the corner of Hardenhuish Estate.

THE VIEW FROM LOWDEN

THE MAIN ROAD in the small village of Lowden to the south-west of Chippenham can be seen in the older photograph (right). Lowden was first recorded in documents in 1249 and probably means 'a hill owned by Lolla'. Lowden, as a small suburb, is often linked to nearby Rowden and originally had its own small village green.

However, when the railway embankment was surveyed it passed through Lowden severely reducing the size of the village centre. The photograph above, which dates to about 1905, shows rows of workers' houses constructed in 1883 and called Lowden Villas. In the far distance can be seen the bell turret of St Peter's church.

WITH THE WIDENING of the road, many of the gardens in Lowden have been reduced, but with its small cottages, it still retains a charming, small village feel.

DALLAS ROAD

BETWEEN THE TWO world wars the area between the railway embankment and Bristol Road was developed in a piecemeal fashion. Dallas Road was constructed in a typical 1930s style with front gabled roofs and bays, much like 1930s housing all over England.

THE BUILDINGS on Dallas Road have changed very little on the whole since their construction in the 1930s, and it is still a quiet and pleasant street. In 1974 a new fire station was built at the end of the road, and it continues to serve the local community in the present day.

Other titles published by The History Press

Wiltshire Folk Tales
KIRSTY HARTSIOTIS

These lively and entertaining folk tales from one of Britain's most ancient counties are vividly retold by local storyteller Kirsty Hartsiotis. Their origins lost in the oral tradition, these thirty stories from Wiltshire reflect the wisdom of the county and its people. Discover the Moonraker's passages and Merlin's trickery, dabchicks and the devil, the flying monk of Malmesbury and a canal ghost story. These tales have all stood the test of time, and remain classic texts that will be enjoyed time and again by modern readers.

978 0 7524 5736 9

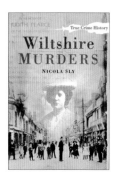

The Wiltshire Regiment 1914–1959
MARTIN MCINTYRE

Focusing on the period between the First World War and 1959, this painstakingly researched book uses over 200 photographs to vividly document the Wiltshire Regiment' role in many campaigns and battles from the trenches on the Western Front to terrorists in Cyprus in 1959, from Shanghai through to the Second World War. Some of the images are intensely moving, some funny, and all are accompanied by detailed text which endeavours to tell the stories behind the images.

978 0 7524 3757 6

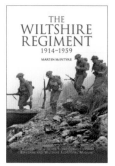

Wiltshire Murders
NICOLA SLY

Contained within the pages of this book are the stories behind some of the most heinous crimes ever committed in Wiltshire. They include the murder of Eliza Jones, stabbed to death by her common-law husband in 1836; the shooting of a policeman in 1892; Mary Ann Nash, who disposed of her illegitimate son in 1907 by dropping him into a disused well; and Edward Richards, who died in Trowbridge during an attempted robbery in 1925. This book will appeal to anyone interested in the shady side of Wiltshire's history.

978 0 7524 4896 1

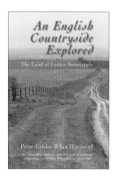

An English Countryside Explored
PETER FOWLER & IAN BLACKWELL

Around 1800 Lettice Sweetapple lived in West Overton, Wiltshire, between Avebury and Marlborough. Her house looked across the River Kennet to the chalk downs and southwards to woods once part of the Savernake Forest. She represents hundreds of thousands of people whose lives were shaped by the changing landscape, and who change it, over ten millennia. In setting out to answer the question 'How has this landscape come to look as it does?' The authors have amassed a fascinating mountain of information.

978 0 7524 5020 9

Visit our website and discover thousands of other History Press books.
www.thehistorypress.co.uk

The
History
Press